Little Mitchie

GROSS BUT TRUE

WEIRD, WILD, AND WONDERFUL

TAMRA B. ORR

CREATING YOUNG NONFICTION READERS

Little Mitchie books spark curiosity and support early nonfiction reading for students in Grades 2-3. Designed to build vocabulary, support second language learners, and prepare readers for middle-grade content, each book includes helpful tips for parents and educators to build confidence and deepen understanding of the world.

TIPS FOR READING NONFICTION WITH BEGINNING READERS

Talk about Nonfiction

Begin by explaining that nonfiction books give us information that is true. The book will be organized around a specific topic or idea, and we may learn new facts through reading.

Look at the Parts

Most nonfiction books have helpful features. Our *Little Mitchie* titles include color photographs and graphic aids, a table of contents, a glossary, and an index. Share the purpose of these features with your reader.

Color Photos and Graphic Aids

A lot of information can be found by "reading" photos, charts, maps, and other graphic aids found within nonfiction texts. Help your reader learn more about the different ways information can be displayed.

Table of Contents

Located at the front of the book, this list shows the big ideas within the text and the page numbers where they can be found.

Glossary

Located at the back of the book, the glossary defines key words and phrases that are related to the topic. These words and phrases can be found in the text in colored type.

Index

Located at the back of the book, an index is an alphabetical list of topics and the page numbers where they can be found.

With a little help and guidance about reading nonfiction, you can feel good about introducing a young reader to the world of *Little Mitchie* nonfiction books.

Little Mitchie is an imprint of:

Mitchell Lane
PUBLISHERS

2001 SW 31st Avenue
Hallandale, FL 33009
mitchelllanepub.com

First Edition, 2027.

Author: Tamra B. Orr
Designer: Jen Bowers
Editor: Tricia Hoffman

Library of Congress Cataloging-in-Publication Data
Title: Gross But True / by Tamra Orr

Description: Hallandale, FL :
Mitchell Lane Publishers, [2027]

Identifiers:
ISBN 979-8-89260-892-3 (library bound)
ISBN 979-8-89260-995-1 (eBook)

Library of Congress Control Number: 2026936396

PHOTO CREDITS
Shutterstock: cover, p.1 ©2019 Aquarius Studio, ©2022 JoanneStrell, p.5 ©2006 Joseph Calev, p.7 ©2023 izzet ugutmen, p.8–9 ©2019 LightField Studios, p.10 ©2020 Jason Busa, p.11 ©2016 Crevis, p.12 ©2012 photolinc, p.13 ©2012 Tom Reichner, p.14 ©2007 Denise Kappa, p.15 ©2016 taveesak srisomthavil, p.16–17 ©2017 Kurit afshen, p.18 ©2017 Comedstock, p.19 ©2019 Brilliant Eye, p.20 ©2019 sruilk, p.21 ©2025 Maliflower73, p.22 ©2025 New Africa, ©2025 Tatiana Foxy, ©2016 Zenzeta, ©2020 Andrii Spy_k

TABLE OF CONTENTS

Chapter One

EWW, GROSS!

There are many beautiful things in life, but some things are—well, let's admit it—gross! Where are they hiding? Get ready to say "Eww!"

CHANGING WITH TIME

What we think of as gross today was once normal! In ancient Rome, people often chatted while they all sat on toilets. **Urine** was used for doing laundry—and even as a mouthwash!

Chapter Two

AROUND THE HOUSE

What do you think is the germiest place in your house? It's not the toilet! It is likely your kitchen sink. Hundreds of types of **bacteria** can grow in wet sponges and dishcloths.

The bathroom does have a lot of ick factors. Millions of bacteria are often hidden in your toothbrush. They come from your mouth and skin. And from all of those flushes with the toilet lid up!

A HARD CALL

One of the germiest items in the house is a cell phone. One study showed that most phones have more than 17,000 types of bacteria. That's 10 times dirtier than the average toilet seat!

Ready to change your sheets? You might be now! Almost all sheets are covered in tiny, **microscopic** pests called dust mites. They live by eating dead skin cells.

Chapter Three

AROUND THE WORLD

A buzzing fly is annoying—but it is also rather gross. Flies carry more than 65 diseases, including **cholera**. Worst of all, when they land on your food, they usually throw up and poop before eating!

SPEAKING OF POO

Turkey vultures stay cool and clean by pooping and peeing on their legs! This helps to cool them down on hot days. The acid in their pee also kills any bacteria they might have on their legs.

Usually flowers smell wonderful, but not the corpse flower. One of the largest flowers in the world smells like rotten meat. Ick! Some **pollinating** insects like that smell. They visit and then carry off pollen!

JUST A TASTE

It looks like a spike-covered football. Cut it open and the smell might remind you of garbage. This is a durian, one of the weirdest tropical fruits in the world. Despite its smell, it tastes sweet.

Vomiting is never fun, but be glad you aren't some frogs. If they eat something **toxic**, they throw up their entire stomachs! Their front legs wipe off any leftover bits. Then, they swallow their stomachs back inside.

Chapter Four

AROUND THE BODY

Humans can also be weird—and gross! For example, think about sneezing. Sneezes remove an **irritant** from our noses. The spray can travel up to 100 miles (161 km) per hour and up to 30 feet (9 m) away!

BETTER OUT THAN IN

Farting can be embarrassing, but it is a very normal thing for humans to do. The average person farts about 14 times a day. It lets out air and gases in the intestinal tract.

HUMAN SHEDDING

Humans have billions of skin cells—which is a good thing, since we shed 30,000 to 40,000 of them every hour! In a year, that adds up to about eight pounds (3.6 kg) of dead skin.

Human mouths produce two pints (1 L) of saliva daily. We lose about 100 hairs a day. Our noses and ears never fully stop growing. Perhaps this means that people are the weirdest, wildest, and most wonderful of all!

EVEN WILDER!

Most of the dust in your home is actually dead human skin.

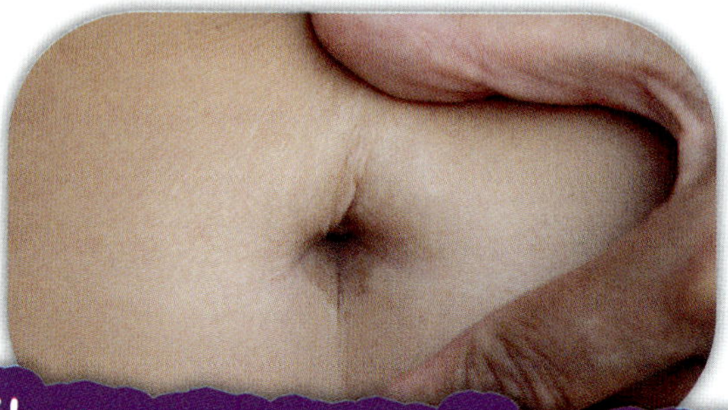

There are more than 2,400 types of bacteria living in your belly button.

People produce 26 gallons (98 L) of sweat in bed every year.

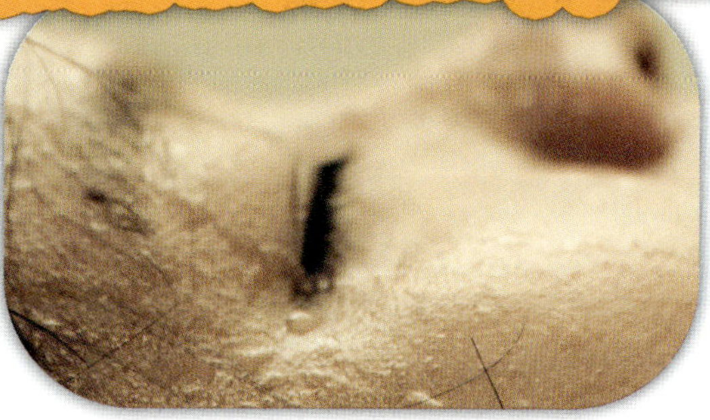

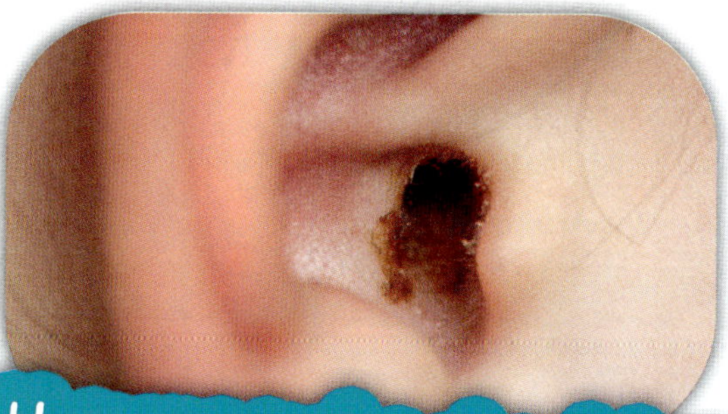

Humans make about two pounds (0.9 kg) of earwax during their lifetimes.

GLOSSARY

bacteria (bak-teer-ee-uh) single-celled organisms found everywhere

cholera (kah-lur-uh) a dangerous disease that causes vomiting and diarrhea

irritant (ir-i-tent) something that causes discomfort

microscopic (mye-kruh-skah-pik) so small it cannot be seen without a microscope

pollinating (pah-luh-nayt-ing) the process of moving pollen from one place to another

toxic (tahk-sik) poisonous

urine (yoor-uhn) yellow pee stored in the bladder

FURTHER READING

DK. *1,000 Amazing Gross Facts.* DK Publishing, 2023.

Ward, Michelle. *The Mega Book of Gross & Funny Facts for Kids.* Harbor & Ink Press, 2025.

Zeitgeist. *Would You Rather? Junior: That's So Gross!* Z Kids, 2025.

ON THE INTERNET

15 Facts About the Human Body!
www.natgeokids.com/uk/discover/science/general-science/15-facts-about-the-human-body/
Learn some cool (and sometimes gross!) things about human's bodies with National Geographic.

229 Fun Facts For Kids—Weird But True!
https://kidpillar.com/fun-facts-for-kids-weird-but-true/
Learn a bunch of random fun facts about the weather, animals, food, humans, sports, and much more.

INDEX